Jesus Was
Way Cool

Jesus
Was Way Cool

John S. Hall

Soft Skull Press
1997

for Yuriko

Selections from "Jesus Was Way Cool" have appeared previously on the following records:

King Missile, KING MISSILE (Atlantic, 1994)
King Missile, HAPPY HOUR (Atlantic, 1992)
John S. Hall & Kramer, REAL MEN (Shimmy Disc, 1991)
King Missile, THE WAY TO SALVATION (Atlantic, 1991)
King Missile, MYSTICAL SHIT (Shimmy Disc, 1990)
King Missile (Dog Fly Religion), THEY (Shimmy Disc, 1988)
King Missile (Dog Fly Religion), FLUTING ON THE HUMP
                                        (Shimmy Disc, 1987)

Photos by Andréa Bucci.

Fourth Edition
March 1997

Soft Skull Press

Sander Hicks   Editor

Susan Mitchell   Design

CONTENTS

Sensitive Artist 1
Take Stuff from Work 3
The Sandbox..........................5
Fish..7
Wuss......................................9
I'm Open 11
The Love Song 13
They 15
How to Remember
          Your Dreams 17
He Needed............................19
Jesus Was Way Cool............21
The Neither World 23
Fourthly................................25
Dinosaurs 27
The Way to Salvation..........29
Life 31
The Indians...........................33
Scotland................................35
To Walk Among the Pigs 37
My Life..................................39
How Much Longer? 41
Wind-Up Toys......................43

Hide the Knives 45

Everybody Screams Inside ... 49

Francis Bacon 51

Sink 53

Martin Scorsese 55

It's Saturday 57

The Evil Children 59

I'm Sorry 61

Happy Hour 63

Love Is 65

What If? 67

Let's Have Sex 69

Delores 71

Socks 73

The Commercial 75

A Good Hard Look 77

Hope 79

The Prophecy 81

Happy Note 85

SENSITIVE ARTIST

I am a sensitive artist. Nobody understands me because I am so deep. In my work, I make allusions to books that nobody else has read, music that nobody else has heard, and art that nobody else has seen. I can't help it because I am so much more intelligent and well-rounded than everyone who surrounds me.

I stopped watching TV when I was six months old because it was so boring and stupid, and started reading books and going to recitals and art galleries. I don't go to recitals any more, because my hearing is too sensitive, and I don't go to art galleries any more because there are people there, and I can't deal with people because they don't understand me.

I stay home, reading books that insult my intelligence, and working on my work, which no one understands. I am sensitive.

TAKE STUFF FROM WORK

Take stuff from work. It's the best way to feel better about your job. Never buy pens or pencils or paper. Take 'em from work. Rubber bands, paper clips, memo pads, folders—take 'em from work. It's the best way to feel better about your low pay and appalling working conditions.

Take an ashtray—they got plenty. Take coat hangers. Take a—take a trash can. Why buy a file cabinet? Why buy a phone? Why buy a personal computer or word processor? Take 'em from work.

I took a whole desk from the last place I worked. They never noticed and it looks great in my apartment. Take an electric pencil sharpener. Take a case of white-out; you might need it one day. It's your duty as an oppressed worker to steal from your exploiters. Take stuff from work. And fuck off on the company time. I wrote this at work. They're paying me to write about stuff I steal from them. Life is good.

THE SANDBOX

And I would go
And I would go every day almost to the sandbox
And 'cause I loved the sandbox so much
And 'cause I had my pail and my shovel
And and my shovel

And I would play in the sandbox
And it would be so fun
And I would make mountains in the sand
And I would have so much fun

And and but one day I went to the sandbox
And it was so sad
And I cried and I cried and I cried, because
Someone took a doody in my sandbox
Someone took a doody in my sandbox

And that was so bad
And that was so disgusting
And how could they do that
And and that was so bad

And and I didn't see it

And and I sat down right in it
And it felt squishy and I got up
And I cried and I cried and I cried

And why didn't they clean up after themselves?
Why didn't they clean up the mess?

And now my pants are dirty
And I'm crying and I'm crying and I'm crying
And I'm never going to the sandbox again
I'm never going to the sandbox again
And I hate everybody.

FISH

And now I would like to speak about fish.
I have never spoken about fish before, at least, not that I can remember.
So now would most certainly be a good time to do so.
After all, there're plenty of fish in the ocean, and fish in time saves nine.
This leads me to my next point.

WUSS

I was a teenage wuss. In junior high school, I had oily, stringy hair and lots of pimples. I wore really wussy clothes. Most of the other kids called me a faggot. Even some of the other wusses called me a faggot. There were maybe five kids in the whole school who were wussier than I was. I was really wussed out.

I was afraid of girls, and guys scared the shit out of me. They used to say to me, "What are you, fucking queer?" They wanted me to fight, to prove I wasn't a faggot. But I didn't fight, I ran away. I was a wuss.

I was never into any sports at all. I never took showers after gym class. I wore my gym clothes under my regular clothes so I wouldn't have to change in front of everybody else. I was afraid to realize my full potential in school because, to the other kids, the smarter you were, the wussier you were and the wussier you were, the more they beat you up.

I was a hopeless wuss. Wuss, wuss, wuss. I was into science fiction and math and chess.

It was not fun being a wuss, and even now, now that I like to think I'm not nearly as much of a wuss as I once was, I still feel kind of wussy from time to time: residual wussiness—the kind of thing you can never really leave behind. That's the way it goes.

I'M OPEN

I'm open
you can enter me
you can exit me
you never have to ask
I'm open
open my head
cut into my head
take the lid off my head
empty out my head
plunge your hands into my open head
take huge handfuls of head stuff
make mudpies
make a sculpture
make a collage of blood and brains
make sweetbread and invite me to dinner
enter me
and exit me
I'm open

THE LOVE SONG

Faces on the walls
invisible faces on the walls
faces of criminals
faces of animals
faces faces faces
all over the walls
telling me to cut up your corpse
telling me to paint in your blood
telling me to slice up your face
the faces on the walls
are telling me to paint in your blood
but I don't listen to them
because I love you

THEY

They can put a man on the moon
They can make soap out of people and food out of wood
They can build machines that do the jobs of millions of human beings
They can feed the entire world
They can go zero to fifty in 3.9 seconds
They can grow oranges in the desert and tomatoes underwater
They can predict or affect the weather sometimes
They can create a disease and then claim it's the cure
They can build superconductors that will permanently alter the way
they live forever
They can make a coffee I like without caffeine
They can blow themselves up or wait for the sun to explode

How to Remember Your Dreams

In order to remember your dreams, you must think of them as if they were little kittens.

When you wake up in the morning, before you get out of bed, sit up and say, "Here, kitty kitty, kitty kitty kitty kitty kitty kitty kitty kitty. Here, kitty kitty, kitty kitty kitty kitty kitty kitty kitty kitty. Here, kitty kitty, kitty kitty kitty kitty kitty kitty kitty kitty. Here, kitty kitty, kitty kitty kitty kitty kitty kitty kitty kitty. Here, kitty kitty, kitty kitty kitty kitty kitty kitty kitty kitty."

If this doesn't work, you must go into the kitchen and pour out a saucer of cream.

Place it by the foot of the bed and say, "Here, kitty kitty, kitty kitty kitty kitty kitty kitty kitty kitty. Here, kitty kitty, kitty kitty kitty kitty kitty kitty kitty kitty. Here, kitty kitty, kitty kitty kitty kitty kitty kitty kitty kitty. Here, kitty kitty, kitty kitty kitty kitty kitty kitty kitty kitty. Here, kitty kitty, kitty kitty kitty kitty kitty kitty kitty kitty. Here, kitty kitty, kitty kitty kitty kitty kitty kitty kitty kitty. Here, kitty kitty, kitty kitty kitty kitty kitty kitty kitty kitty."

When the kitty gets the cream, the dream is remembered.

HE NEEDED

He needed more time
He needed more space
He needed more money
He needed more friends
He needed more music
He needed more food
He needed more drugs
He needed more color
He needed more sex
He needed more mass
He needed more height
He needed more pull
He needed more slack
He needed to stop jerking around and get his stuff together
He needed a job
He needed a new direction
He needed religion
He needed a television set
He needed some good advice
He needed discipline
He needed discipline
He needed discipline
He needed a ticket on the next train out of town

He needed to try harder
He needed less pressure on him
He needed a tissue
He needed to go to the bathroom
He needed to chatter incessantly
He needed to ponder universal themes
He needed to wax poetic
He needed an audience
He needed a dancing partner
He needed new clothing
He needed a place to run to
He needed to feel that he was getting in the way of progress
He needed a dog
He needed to get his apartment cleaned
He needed to write a grocery list
He needed to paint
He needed a way out

JESUS WAS WAY COOL

Jesus was way cool. Everybody liked Jesus.
Everybody wanted to hang out with him.
Anything he wanted to do, he did.
He turned water into wine, and if he had wanted to,
He could have turned wheat into marijuana, sugar into cocaine, or
vitamin pills into amphetamines.
He walked on the water and swam on the land.
He would tell these stories and people would listen.
He was really cool.
If you were blind, or lame, you just went to Jesus and he would put his
hands on you and you would be healed.
That's so cool.

He could have played guitar better than Hendrix.
He could have told the future.
He could have baked the most delicious cake in the world.
He could have scored more goals than Wayne Gretzky.
He could have danced better than Baryshnikov.
Jesus could have been funnier than any comedian you can think of.

Jesus told people to eat his body and drink his blood.
That's so cool. Jesus was so cool.
But then some people got jealous of how cool he was, so they killed him.

But then he rose from the dead! He rose from the dead, did a little dance, and went up to heaven. I mean, that's so cool. Jesus was so cool. No wonder there are so many Christians.

THE NEITHER WORLD

In the Neither World, Every Thing is Versed and Reversed.
The Neither World Contains and Corrects all Contradictions.
All Division Collapses into Itself, into Unity.

Forever is Never in the Neither World.
To Connect is to Sever.
All is One is Several is None.

The Foundation is in the Abyss.
The Truth is the Lamb is the Fish.
The Key is in the Sunlight in the Window.

The Virgin Chases the Moon.
The Lamb is Slaughtered and We All Drink the Blood.
We All Drink the Blood in the Neither World of Sameck.

FOURTHLY

Firstly, you begin.
Secondly, you continue.
Thirdly, you end.
Fourthly,

DINOSAURS

There used to be dinosaurs
There used to be dinosaurs walking around the earth
Bigass brontosaurus
Eating trees and small animals
Bend down, eat a goat
Bend down, drink a lake
Bend down, I don't know
About the dinosaurs
What do I know about the dinosaurs
Get real

Would I have more to say if I didn't have a phone?
Would my life look like eggplant toupee Aunt Jemimah stuffing mix?
Would Cary Granite and Stony Curtis be a part of my rock & roll fantasy?
Would the pillsbury doughboy step on glass and giggle?
Fuck you! I wanna know!

Would the dogs be barking in barbershop quartets when mama stands
on the porch crying "Come home now son, it's the apocalypse, come
on home?"
Would it be the end, would it really be the end, or would it start all
over again?
Time to learn the mongoose dance

Time to talk to people and hear what they say
Time for clear thought
Opossum pudding pie pops
A vast assortment of new products for the home and office

And will there be chandelier burgers?
And will there be pretzels and hot dogs for everyone, and glow in the
dark pork and beans avec arroz y con pollo?
Will the sky turn white in the middle of the night?
And when will I be loved?
Is this my beginning or is this the end?
Are the dinosaurs exploding, are they rising out of the earth to replace
Dan Rather and Charlemagne?

I wanna know
about the dinosaurs
I don't know about the dinosaurs
Dinosaurs
Dinosaurs

THE WAY TO SALVATION

"Spare the Goats and Spoil the Lambs!" screamed the Farm Man, "It's raining fireballs and boulders and radioactive debris."

"Run for your life and kill your wife," cried the Preacher, "It's the end of the Christian Era."

"You'll never make it; no need to fake it," giggled the Antichrist, "Just put on an Otis Redding records and start the dance."

"Open up the windows and let the fresh air out!" said the Television to the Shackled Children, "This is the Way to Salvation."

LIFE

Life,
with its wonderful smells,
with its enchanting plant life,
with its exhilarating animal life,
with its perplexing micro-orgasmic life
and so on.

Life,
with its amazing sensations,
with its scintillating sounds,
with its vivacious visions,
with its yummy tastes,
and so on.

Life,
with its natural elements,
its unnatural elements,
and all of its other elements,
and so on.

Life,
with its death,
with its birth,

with its girth,
with its earth
with its stars and its bars and its buildings
and poison and power and flowers and showers and children and viruses
and get rich quick schemes
and all that other life stuff
and soon and so forth
and so on

This is life the one you get so go and have a ball
This is life,
don't worry,
it will kill you,
don't worry,
it's delicious,
don't worry,
it'll all be over sooner than Shiva can open an eye.

THE INDIANS

The Indians lived all over this land before we came and killed them. That was very bad of us. We thought we needed the land, but for the most part, we just ruined it anyway, and now, nobody can use it. That's the way we are. We're pigs.

One of my favorite foods to eat is called corn. The Indians call it maize. We call the Indians "Indians." This is because Columbus thought he was in India when he first came to this land.

Some people say we should call the Indians "Native Americans," because they were here in America before us, but before us, this land wasn't called America. It was named America by a mapmaker who never even came here. He lived in Europe and made maps and when he found out about this land, he just made a map of it, and just put his name on it, 'cause he could. That's the way we are. We're pigs.

As I was writing this, a cockroach fell from the sky and onto the table. I killed it, because I did. That's the way I am. This doesn't really have very much to do with the Indians, though. I guess I kind of got sidetracked. Anyway, I hope you see my point.

SCOTLAND

I'd like to go to Scotland
I'd like to wear a kilt
I'd like to show off my two legs
And do just what I wilt

I'd like to go to Scotland
And show off my two thighs
I'd like to wear a mini-kilt
And poke you in the eyes

I'd like to go to Scotland
And be so very bad
And wear a micro-mini-kilt
Of plaid

TO WALK AMONG THE PIGS

To walk among the pigs
To go where the pigs go and do as the pigs do
To inhale the pungent stench of the pigs and truly savor the scent
To sing the song of the pigs
To build up a rapport, to be one with the pigs
To work shoulder to shoulder with the pigs on pig-like projects
To sweat like a pig and then to realize that pigs never sweat
To wallow in the mud with the pigs
To experience absolutely all that pigness entails
To hear, To see, To feel like a pig
To think, eat and smell like a pig
To comprehend completely what it is to be a pig
To fully understand that you and the pigs and all other things in the
universe are of the same ilk
And then...
To weed out all non-pig things, to fully cultivate and allow to blossom
the flower that is the pig within your soul
And to finally stand alone, in the garden of the Absolute and pray and
prey and pray like a pig

MY LIFE

My life as a cloud
My life as a bowl of ashes
My life as a plate of onion soup
My life as a string of poloponies
My life as a singing waiter
My life as an insufferable bore
My life as an overdue library book
My life as a new way to be
My life as a brand new car
My life as a private detective
My life as a way to get to Springfield Massachusetts
My life as a coloring book
My life as a bush of ghosts
My life as a Buddhist monk
My life as a pair of Shirley McLaine's pantyhose
My life as a set of matching luggage
My life as a new car
My life as the horsehead nebula
My life as a teenage lobotomy
My life as an inflatable love doll
My life as an end to all things
My life as a new beginning
Take my life
Take my life
Take my life
I'm not using it

HOW MUCH LONGER?

I want the car to explode when you drive me to the K-mart.
I want you to solder my face to the mighty oak tree.
I want to fuck myself with my atom bomb.
Why is it that I cannot, not even only once, find glass in my dinner or
razor blades in the bedsheets?
I pay my taxes.
When will my hard work and dedication pay off?
When will I reap what I have sown?
When will my tiny penis shrivel up and disappear?
When will my testicles bleed with joy?
When will I drown in urine and vomit and my menstrual juices?
I want to be the lamb slaughtered in the Milk Bar.
I want to live.
I want to live.
I want to die.
I want to live.
How much longer must I wait?

WIND-UP TOYS

If most of us were wind-up toys, could we trust the few of us that weren't to wind us up when necessary?

I think not. We would be a separate oppressed minority, even if we were in the majority, it would still be that way.

The ones that weren't wind-up toys would have the upper hand, and we would have to look out for each other, because they wouldn't.

They would only wind up those that they saw fit, those that conformed to their ways.

If most of us were wind-up toys, it would be in our interest to learn how to wind ourselves up, or each other up.

That's reality.
That's the way it is.

HIDE THE KNIVES

It's a day of sun and rice
It's a day of days and roses
It's a day of gray and holy
It's a day of dates and raisins
It's a day of nuclear sandwich pie
It's a day of fluorescent tomatoes
It's a day of cantaloupes highways
It's a day of tornado surprise
It's a day to ask the doorman, "Pardon me, what day is it? Can I use
your car? Mine needs a new bandaid, it has a hole in it."
It's a day to hide the knives
Hide the knives
Hide the knives
I can't think straight
It's such a beautiful moonbeam banana day
That I can hardly stand it
Hide the knives, this is it
Hide the knives, I really mean it this time
Hide the knives, I can't think
And all I see is white white pain light
It's a beautiful day and there is no time
There is no time but the present
There is no future
And there's never been a past
Hide the knives and let's go bowling

Hide the knives and put the cat out for the night
Hide the knives and let's see if this is the right kind of household appliance
Hide the knives so I can split my head open with a pickax instead of carving myself up like the thanksgiving doughboy
Hide the knives and you and I and everybody will be safe for another few seconds
Hide the knives and hold me down and slap me hard and spank me and spank me and spank me
I am so bad
Hide the knives 'cause my wrists are already bleeding
Hide the knives 'cause I've already cut my prick off
Hide the knives 'cause today is such a beautiful day and I can't go outside and I can't be alone with you
Hide those knives kids, and if you order now you get a free bamboo steamer and a fondue set
Hide the knives, tie me up, and gag me and throw me into the Gowanus canal, I love the water, the water is so beautiful, the way it reflects the sun in your hair, the light in your eyes;
The birds are so beautiful, life is so wonderful, I'm going to implode, expand, contract, negate,
It's happening, it's happening, it's over,
And I wonder where you are and I haven't got a clue
The game is over. Please pass the knives. It's over. It was Colonel Mustard in the billiard room with the revolver.

It's over. The game is over. Put the knives away and return to your seat and await further instructions. Pancreas.

EVERYBODY SCREAMS INSIDE

So here it is: another day of days:
Time marches on like a soldier into cattle,
The lawnmower flies past my window, and
The children are nonplused.
The pants are pressed and ready for action.
There's a Barbie Doll at the bottom of the well,
And the milkshake of despair shakes hands
With secret agent 666.
The relentless, humid sun beats down,
baking the earth into piping hot brickcake, as
blueberries burst like lip balms.
My great-great-great grandmother grieves and cries at
The sight of the bunnies hopping and bopping about the backyard,
beating each other to death with peacock feathers.
And then, like the second coming of Krishna,
A single snowflake falls to earth,
And everybody screams inside.

FRANCIS BACON

I was reading a Colin Wilson book
Where it said that Francis Bacon said
That the human mind is easily fooled
That we believe what we want to believe
And recognize only those facts
That conform to those beliefs

Now a lot of people say Francis Bacon
Wrote the Shakespeare plays
In addition to making all those really cool paintings
In The Tempest, Act One Scene Two
It says:
"Begun to tell me what I am but stopt"—that's the first line
"And left me to a bootless inquisition"—that's the second line
And the third line:
"Concluding stay: not yet."

Get it?
Begun begins with a "B"
And And begins with an "A"
Concluding begins with "C-O-N"
B-A-C-O-N. Bacon!

Also, on the back cover of King Lear,
Shakespeare isn't wearing any shoes
And he's facing the wrong way
It seems pretty obvious to me, but what do I know?

I heard maybe he wrote the King James Bible, too.
There are three verses in Exodus
One after the other
Each with 72 letters each
And if you stack them on top of each other
And write the second one backwards while standing on a chair
It sounds like "cranberry sauce"
Now Shakespeare says it was just a drawing
That Julian had brought home from school
But I don't believe that for a minute

I don't know what to believe any more.

SINK

Holy holy holy holy
All is holy in the sink
In the sinking all is holy
Holy holy down the sink

Holy holy sinking down
Holy sinking down the hole
Down the sinking holy holy
Sinking holy holy down

Holy holy all is holy
All is holy down the sink
In the sinking all is holy
All is holy in the hole
Down the holy holy sinking
All is holy in the sink
Sinking down the holy sinking
All is sinking down the hole

Sink sink sink sink sink
Sinking down the holy down
Holy sinking down the sinking
Sinking holy down the sink

Holy holy holy sinking
All is sinking down the holy
Holy holy all is sinking
All is sinking All is sinking

Sink Sink Sink Sink Sink
Sink Sink Sink Sink Sink
Sink Sink Sink Sink Sink
Sink Sink Sink Sink Sink

Holy Sinking
Sinking down the hole

MARTIN SCORSESE

He makes the best fucking films
He makes the best fucking films
If I ever meet him, I'm gonna grab his fucking neck and just shake him
and say "Thank you. Thank you. Thank you for making such excellent
fucking movies."
Then I'm gonna twist his nose all the way the fuck around
And then rip off one of his ears and throw it like a, like a, like a fucking
frisbee
I wanna chew his fucking lips off and grab his head and suck out one of
his eyes and chew on it and spit it out and say "Thank you, thank you,
for all of your fucking films."
Then I'm gonna pick him up by the hair
swing him over my head a few times
and throw him across the room and kick all his fucking teeth in and
then stomp on his face forty or fifty times
'cause he makes the best fucking films
he makes the best fucking films I've ever seen in my life
I fucking love him
I fucking love him

IT'S SATURDAY

I want to be different, like everybody else I want to be like
I want to be just like all the different people
I have no further interest in being the same, because I have seen
difference all around, and now I know that that's what I want

I don't want to blend in and be indistinguishable,
I want to be a part of the different crowd,
and assert my individuality along with others
who are different like me

I don't want to be identical to anyone or anything
I don't even want to be identical to myself

I want to look in the mirror and wonder,
"Who is that person? I've never seen that person before.
I've never seen anyone like that before."
I want to call into question the very idea that identity can be attached
I want a floating, shifting, ever-changing persona
Invisibility and obscurity,
detachment from the ego and all of its pursuits.
Unity is useless
Conformity is competitive and divisive and leads only to stagnation
and death.

If what I'm saying doesn't make any sense,
that's because sense can not be made
It's something that must be sensed
And I, for one, am incensed by all of this complacency
Why oppose war only when there's a war?
Why defend the clinics only when they're attacked?
Why support the squats and the parks only when the police come to
close them down?
Why are we always reactive?
Let's activate something
Let's fuck shit up
Whatever happened to revolution for the hell of it
Whatever happened to protesting nothing in particular, just protesting
'cause it's Saturday and there's nothing else to do?

THE EVIL CHILDREN

And so
The very evil children
Took the dog out to play in the park

Then they took him home
And refused
To set him on fire

They were evil, evil, evil children
And they refused to do
As they were told

They would say,
"Why should we leave the elderly woman
In the middle of the Expressway?
Fuck you, we're not doing it."

Then they would go downstairs
And prepare
The Molotov cocktails,

Knowing full well
That when they were finished,

There was no way in hell
They were gonna blow up
The neighbors' barn
They were evil, evil, evil children.

All their lives,
People expected them to do bad.
They almost
Never delivered †

†Last verse stolen from Roger Manning.

I'm Sorry

No, I never was in Vietnam
I never once dove into an empty swimming pool
I never let the carpet walk right out from under me
I never painted a house or a tree
I never did become an exotic dancer, or a customer service representative
I never took the pulse of a dying duck, or gave mouth to mouth resuscitation to a horsefly
In a way, I suppose you could say that my experience is quite limited
For example, I never locked Oliver Cromwell in a broom closet while singing Waltzing Matilda
I never sawed a television in half, although I once saw Wendy O. Williams saw a guitar
I never played a decent game of jacks
I never played poker with a toothless one-eyed pirate who kept picking his teeth with a bowie knife to distract me, while his parrot looked over my shoulder and told him what cards I had by using an elaborate code involving vomiting, chirping, and sea chanteys
I never bought a lamp—wait—I did buy a lamp once
But I never bought a lantern, or a lambskin prophylactic
I never bought lima beans or lime pudding
I never bought a lion or a Lionel Richie album
I never bought anything beginning with the letter "L" except lollipops, light bulbs and lettuce—and the lamp

I never laid down for a nap and found the Everly Brothers in bed
with me
I never let a cyborg take out the garbage

I'm sorry
I stole the radio
I did it
I sawed the legs off the periodic table
I re-elected the president
I did it, it was my fault
I farted in the church
I'm sorry
I did many many bad things and I am so sorry

HAPPY HOUR

In this happy sing song hell hole
In this torture house of glee
In this perfect playpen prison
There's so much to do and see

On this euthanasia morning
Colorful carnival of pain
Let us drink delicious poison
If they won't let us, let's complain

Genetic engineers
Crucified our sacred hymns
While flesh fell off our bodies
And we lost our limbs

LOVE IS

Love is beautiful
Like birds that sing
Love is not ugly
Like rats
In a puddle of vomit

Love is beautiful
Like the sunshine
And the dancing wind
Love is not ugly
Like pus
And lice
And tobacco snot
Love is beautiful

Love is beautiful
Like all the little animals
In a forest full of green
That smells like pine
And wonder
Love is not invisible brain control
And pain
And malicious intent

And lying all the time
Although it can be all of these things
And more

Love is a many-splendoured thing
It is not a shitload of slaughtered pigs
Rotting and festering
In the bleating desert

Love is what love is
And love is not
What love is not

WHAT IF?

One day
What if one day
What if I said
I wish I was a tree
And then, suddenly,
I was a tree!
Then could I wish myself back?
No, trees can't wish

What if I wished I was a wishing tree, a tree that could wish?
What if I wished I was a toilet bowl, and then I was one, and the wind
changed and I stayed that way?

Or what if I wished I was a toilet bowl
And suddenly I was a tree!
Would I be able to say,
"Hey! I wanted to be a toilet bowl, not a tree!?"
No, I wouldn't be able to say that,
Because trees can't talk
They don't have any mouths.
I would have to have the foresight to say,
"I wish I was a toilet,
But if by chance I'm turned into a tree instead, I wish to be a tree with

a mouth that can wish to be changed back into a human being."

Because I'd only ever want to be a toilet or a tree for a very brief period of time.
I guess this is the exact reason why they always say you should be very careful what you wish for.

LET'S HAVE SEX

I will slur
And heel and hem and haw
I will eat a monkey paw
When you call me up and command me to come over to your house
for sex and tea biscuits, I shall clandestinely drop my cummerbund
down the dumbwaiter chute.
Lutes will serenade us like liquid lemonade.
You will glisten like newborn snow, and I will listen like a clairvoyant
nipple clamp.
It will be sex, like nobody has ever had it before in the history of post-
modern lovemaking.
It will be sex, even if it isn't.
It will be sex, even if only in theory, even if it's only pantomime,
even if it's just a memory, or a dream or a symphonic approximation;
after a summer of autonomous sodomy and national geographic spe-
cials about pretty animals that use other little animals as food,
by killing them,
and eating them,
on television.
But we shouldn't even watch television, we should just have sex:
Epoch making, earth shaking,
Teeth chattering, dish clattering,
Fish frying, eye popping,

69

Never stopping, bunny hopping,
Toe tapping, Joseph Papping sex.
Shakespeare in the park kinda sex.
D train ride to Coney Island vacation kinda sex.
Clandestine in the airplane laboratory kind of sex,
Olympic marathon sex,
All the different ways that we feel like having sex, we should,
until we grow old and bored and disillusioned.
Then let us rekindle our feelings,
forget our despair and our celibate nonsense
and fuck like bunnyrats till the cows come home to roost.
so call me sometime, and let's have sex.

DELORES

The air was breathing but I nearly suffocated in my sarcophagus
Where the antelopes wear underwear on their antlers:
On my mantle, memories recede, but cost of living adjustments dance
the Charleston at the Roseland of resplendent nostalgia:

The walls are dripping, and tonight the faces are on the ceiling, and
they are suspiciously silent:
There was a fire tonight, when the sleeping window cracked open a
velvet weathervane as if it was a world weary smile:
There was a pillow plummeting like invisible carbon in a passion play:

If this is only going from A to B and back again, how come when I
clothes my eyes,
I see bedsprings and excrement in deep focus:
Dirty deals that only I am privy to, elegant cobblestone goblets, bone
orchard china, parsnips and lichen:

Puke on me, Delores:
Are you married or a lesbian, are you a celibate Buddhist acolyte, or
are you just detached and unavailable like me:
More to the point where are you: where were you:
I went to the high school reunion, and Delores, there was no puke:

It's a sad lonely song in the barnyard, 'cause Delores ain't sick to her
stomach no more:

SOCKS

LOOK AT ALL MY SOCKS
OH SO MANY MANY SOCKS
I CAN'T EVEN BELIEVE IT
CAN YOU IMAGINE HAVING SO MANY SOCKS?

I CAN'T EVEN BEGIN TO COUNT THEM ALL
LET ALONE EVEN THINK ABOUT WEARING THEM
SO MANY SOCKS
HOW DID I GET SO MANY?
WHERE DID THEY COME FROM
HEY!
WHY DO I HAVE SO MANY SOCKS?

I'm inundated
I can't—
No, I'm sorry
This won't do
I cannot have this
This is too many
I cannot have this many socks
Please take some of these socks immediately away at once

Ah, yes

That is much better
Thank you
This is much more manageable
This is quite good
This is quite precisely the quintessentially right number
I am extremely pleased
Thank you

THE COMMERCIAL

Lately, I've seen red, I've tasted blood, I've killed with words, I've wished and hoped and swam through a river of snot twice as wide as the mighty Mississippi, but I wanna know about the commercial I saw on TV:

An Irish guy walking through a field of green, whistling one of those Irish jigs, and a woman walks up and says, "Manly yes, but I like it too." Then the guy pulls out a huge knife and cuts off his first two fingers, and somehow catches them, in what's left of his left hand, and hands them to the woman. Did I mention they're both dressed in green?

Then they both sing this song together: "Are ya icky are ya sticky are ya hot as anything? Hey cut off two of your fingers, and stab yourself in the eye." Then he stabs himself in the eye, and hands her the knife, and she stabs herself in the eye! Okay? So what about that?

Then they join arms and do this Irish folk dance while taking turns dismembering each other. This was a commercial for deodorant, I think, or soap or something.

So now all the body parts are lying in a heap, but the heads are still singing, "Are ya icky are ya sticky are ya hot as anything? Hey! Get away from summer, and cut off all of your limbs!"

Then all of the body parts start hopping and bopping around, like little bunny rats, then they jump into the mouths of the singing heads, but then they just slip right back out through the severed necks and keep bopping about.

It's very beautiful music that's playing—there's an Irish flute, and a mandolin, I think, and the background singers sound just like the Clancy Brothers. It's really a wonderful commercial, spectacular, it must have cost a fortune to make. The kind of commercial you'd see during the Super Bowl, maybe, where the advertising time costs a million dollars for half a minute. Wow, imagine that, a million dollars for half a minute!

Anyway, by the end of it, it looks like the two of them have been through a juicer, or a food processor or a blender or something: it's just a pink puree of blood, bone and flesh in a big bucket, but it's still singing somehow, "Are ya icky, are ya sticky, are ya hot as anything? Hey! Blend yourself process yourself become a glass of animal juice! Haven't you had enough of fruit juices and vegetable juices? Next time company comes over, offer them a cool refreshing glass of animal juice, offer them a glass of yourself. Give of yourself, stop being such a self-ish piece of snot, okay? Okay? Okay? And now, back to our program..."

A Good Hard Look

I think it's time
We so-called sensitive men
Stopped kidding ourselves,
With all this crap
About how guys in the marines, and garage mechanics
And just generally, you know, macho guys,
About how they're insecure about their masculinity because they have
little dicks:
Because that's crap, and we know it.

Guys in the military, construction workers, football players,
They have bigger dicks than you and I
And we might as well just accept it,
Because it's stupid and dishonest for us to go around implying that us
literary, intellectual, politically aware feminist-type men
Are actually more confident than the insensitive sexist brute type men
Because size doesn't matter, and even if it did,
We have the bigger dicks, because this is bullshit.

I think it's high time we all took a good hard look at our dicks and
faced the music. Ask yourself if your dick is as big as, say, that guy
who beat you up in high school who is now married to some absurdly
attractive woman that you're too enlightened to admit you lust

after, and who would never give you the time of day, because stupid as you might think she is, she's smart enough to know how little your dick is, she's smart enough to know that that guy who beat the shit out of you in high school and would beat the shit out of you again in a second, has a much bigger dick and is a much better lay than you could ever hope to be.

So just admit it
You'll feel better once you accept it,
I admit it, I accept it,
And I'm not about to watch basketball games on television, or join the army, or vote Republican, just for the sake of a few extra inches
Forget it
It's not worth it.
It's just not worth it.

HOPE

And the green man knew.
the green man knows, he'll tell you,
throw it at him and he'll throw it right back to you.

he's ostrich, he'll turn you blue without feathers,
hope is not a book by Woody,
hope is a muscle
hope is not just a word,
no word is just a word,
else why have it be a word at all,
if there is meaning in any thing
there must be meaning in every thing, which would explain why a
Buddhist can stare at a lake or a pebble or a tree for longer than you
can stare at a television, no matter what might be on.

And I don't mean you, or me, but I do:
I mean, everybody: we all want to stay asleep,
conjuring up horrifying image after image,
frightening ourselves into further inertia,
just generating more justification for not getting out of bed,
I don't mean to be preachy,
but what if we were on to something?
I'm not, but what if?

Then, I'd be even more boring,
bumbling and fumbling,
hoping to stumble upon a truth by accident,
the way you might walk along the gutter,
looking down, habitually, forgetting why you do it, until you see the
two crisp twenty dollar bills,
gleaming in the afternoon sun, saying pick me up and use me! spend
me, distribute me, give me away like candy,
I think that is what hope is
hope is about how you found it once,
and then you keep looking,
'cause maybe one day, you'll find it again.

THE PROPHECY

Thank you. There were all around friendly ones, they have guns with anger and they took turns and exchanged shifts in the subway hoping for a dog tie in telekinetic toenail broth

And when they presented their arms to the soup man and told him of the overthrow plan where simple drain pipe pillows washed over an angry mob of screaming leftovers, sizzling and chanting for the freedom of the sky rink,

The soup man took umbrage and ran back inside to tell on them, singing ladle ladle; thy kingdom come, kiss me on the bum, have a stick of gum,

The throng continued to amass outside, and within the circumference, inner circles accumulated and plotted in graphic detail the exact nature of their diametrical opposition, then they ate pi,

And when all the irrational numbers had been engulfed, swallowed up in the spontaneous mass, even the innocent little children began to join in the chorus of hate,

And a beautiful sound was heard upon the great lawn as the genuine counter revolution began to assert itself on closed circuit television,

and in portable hair dryers and short wave radios and microwave ovens
and telekinetic magicians and psychic channelers and funnel cakes,

And funeral processions were stopped dead in their tracks as the
corpses climbed out of their coffins and did an evil skeleton dance
while playing xylophone medleys on each other's decaying bones,

And the great matriarch descended from the sky to chastise the soup
man for letting his ingredients run loose among the hungry, for he too
would be implicated in the show trial,

And when the fallen were brought before the grand tribunal, all the
hosiery of the earth witnessed the mockery of justice and the draconian
outcome, and no one spoke out, not out of fear but out of relief,

And a great baldness uncovered the land as all life blew a heavy sigh,
and the people forgave themselves and went on about their business in
the dog food factories and cannibal malls

And coercion committees convened in hideaway palaces to mete out
the sentences and everyone partook in equal portions of the body and
blood of the brave traitors,

But the great belly of the universe began to rumble and grumble and all could hear the message and fear swept over the unchosen as the fornicators and the insane trampled over the hypocrites and baby savers,

For the great day came and the unborn and the just born swelled into a mighty avenging angel and all were smote indiscriminately, for they were all with sin and they never had the hope they had hoped to have had, and verily, they had prayed to the wrong burger joint,

And they all wailed out "Burger King Burger King Burger King," but it was too late, the king was mad and angry and he sent down a cloud of processed cheese food that engulfed the hungry and the blind, and their hairstyles were made fun of by the fashion queens of the west,

And yet, in all the carnage, a flower asserted itself against the rubble and revolt and spoke in a mighty falsetto, "I am the daisy of redemption, lick my petals and ye too shall breathe eternal fire and nitrous oxide."

And many did follow the flower and flowed into and unto the eternal stream of urine, and they were neither angered nor drunken with joy, they were blissed and blessed and saved,

And Junior said, "Boy am I hungry, Dad, are there any more tofu donuts in the air sickness bag?"

And Dad said, "Here Junior, here Junior, take and eat, do this in resemblance of me."

And Junior said, "O Daddy O Daddy O Daddy O Daddy, this is the best Christmas ever!"

HAPPY NOTE

I don't know why
I'm always inclined
To end on a happy note
Though the point may be mute
Like a ten year old boy
With his throat
And his dreams
Ripped out by wolves

Soft Skull Press

★ ★ ★ Vanguard Press of the Lower East Side ★ ★ ★

"For more on the current state of music-as-art and its struggle for survival in the entertainment business, check out *Online Diaries: the Lollapalooza '95 Tour Journals*, a new pocket-sized book from Soft Skull Press.

The book is worthwhile mostly because Thurston Moore is a good rock critic. Moore reports on Courtney Love punching Kathleen Hanna, Siouxsie Sioux getting drunk backstage and insulting hippies in the midst of mourning the death of Jerry Garcia, learning at the tour's end that Love enjoyed parking privileges the other bands did not ('I related this incident to Beck and he nearly foamed at the mouth he became so enraged') and a lot of other stuff. Best of all, Moore posted in his journal reactions to Lolla from Matador jéfe Gerard Cosloy ('The tour is owned and operated by a consortium of booking agent/mgmt./record co. folks, plus Perry...') and a furious Steve Albini ('What the fuck did you expect...If you choose to fuck a pig in the ass, don't complain that your dick smells like shit come morning.')"

Adam Heimlich
New York Press
October 8, 1996

"The tour journal eliminated the rock critic middle man and created a direct, living and breathing, multiple-perspective story-telling that couldn't have been done by a newspaper, magazine, radio or television."

From the Introduction by Aaron Naparstek

online diaries
The Lollapalooza '95 Tour Journals
of Beck, Courtney Love, Stephen Malkmus, Thurston Moore,
Lou Barlow, Mike Watt, & David Yow

With an INTRODUCTION by Aaron Naparstek Edited by SPINonline

"A scathing take on Lollapalooza."
Sam Pratt, *New York Post*

Road Movies
Lee Ranaldo

"This book reminds me a lot of his work in Sonic Youth. The emptiness of desert towns speaks from an eternal place instead of being hollow, the secrets of the world revealed through radio static...I feel strangely relieved yet wanting more."

M. Halchin, *Bleeding Velvet Octopus*

"*Road Movies*...is like mountain climbing in Boulder. You look around, there's a patch of sky, a woman on your arm, love in bloom, a collage of meadows and sunflowers. No noise just the serenity of Mr. Ranaldo's passing visions. Lee Ranaldo, a là Kerouac, takes us along for the ride, on the road."

Linda Wolfe, *BBGun*

I've been given a glass eye
a hollow telescope
the pavement view
a shadow forming
across fields rushing
through me to you

from
Telescope/Timeshift

New, expanded edition available now, $8.

RAVEN DAYS
Cynthia Nelson

CUSH
Todd Colby

Raven Days by Cynthia Nelson with art-work from Tara Jane is a fresh blast of female gusto. The writing is loose but not slack, melodious but not sweet, bourbon-stained but not sad.

"Cynthia Nelson is a great poet...she radiates an incredible edge and does not dawdle."

Eileen Myles, *PAPER*

"Startling and wonderful to read."
Ron Saah, *Uno Mas*

"A newjack quasimodo!"
M. Doughty, Soul Coughing

"Mr. Colby makes serious sport of lan-guage, showing its basis in the body's impulses and its mutable meanings."

Ann Powers, *The New York Times*

Terra Firma, U.S.A.
Jordan Green

The story of a young punk skateboarding and working as a tobacco stripper in Kentucky.

"A powerful, plotless book...fully formed...serene."
Uno Mas Magazine

Lake Success
Matt Kohn

"He's like Estelle Getty on "The Golden Girls"—the screening mechanism has long since faded, and he's speaking truths and spinning disturbing humor."
David Kirschenbaum, *Boog Lit*

For Conifer Fanatics
Jen Robinson

"Like Ann Magnuson, Jen's writing is oddly funny, witty and just well-traveled."
M. Halchin, *Bleeding Velvet Octopus*

Cash Cow & Artanimal
Sander Hicks
"A recognizable ear for the idiocies of modern language."
Archie Borders, *Louisville Courier-Journal*

Angelus Novus

a novel by Morgan Meis

A post-Frankfurt School Marxist love story. A breakfast nook, a mother, a machine. The novel Morgan Meis wrote before becoming the New School's Graduate Faculty Philosophy Journal Editor.

Ripsnort

poems by Todd Colby

"YOU CAUGHT THE BULL BY THE HORNS
YOU STOOD NEXT TO THE RIVER
YOU LIFTED THE BULL BY THE HORNS OVER
THE FENCE NEXT TO THE RIVER
YOU TOSSED THE BULL INTO THE WATER
BY THE HORNS
YOU WANTED THE BULL THE FUCK OUT
AND NOW IT'S THE FUCK OUT
IT'S A LONG WAY TO TOSS A BULL
BUT YOU DID IT
YOU TOOK IT BY THE HORNS
I HOPE YOU'RE HAPPY."

from "BULL BY THE HORNS"

Where To?

a short story anthology

"New voices, new ideas, new styles; a boldness that comes from confidence. Not your father's anthology. This is the future and the future is affecting, well-written and highly entertaining."

—*Koen Review*

Not Sisters

poems by Cynthia Nelson and
Maggie Nelson

"This has to be one of the most vivdly intense books I've read in a quite a while. It actually feels like a series of short films with all the vibrant energy bouncing past my head. If Soft Skull's other publications are even half as good as this, I want every damn thing they've ever released."

—*Bleeding Velvet Octopus*

Our Mission

Soft Skull Press is the publisher of the New Book. This present moment in history is unique, for although the technology is rapidly changing, the era's political/philosophical discourse can't seem to keep up. At Soft Skull, we wish to seize the initiative and create a new kind of text. Our books reflect a robust critique of power, a curiosity about how the new technologies will impact traditional media relations, and a love for a good read.

We publish sweet, sharp, radically intelligent writers. We get our values from the love of language and confrontation in performance poetry, especially the stuff from the independent music scene.

Soft Skull Press publishes with William Blake's love for the craft. We started out as copiers, in the high-stress "Post-Industrial Era." In an age of declining worker empowerment, one has an obligation to reinvent one's relations to the means of production. We gained access to high-end copying technology as a byproduct of low wages. This makes sense, as it is the ones working with rapidly changing technologies who know how to adapt life to its potentials.

But Soft Skull has outgrown its copy-shop roots. Now, we wish to give back to this world, to take a stand for broadening the range of values of the dominant culture, and to universally enrich life.

sample free text from the vanguard press: www.softskull.com

Forthcoming from Soft Skull, 1997:

Oscar Caliber Gun
Henry Baum

"Fast-paced, funny, intense, insane! A fine debut from H. Baum."

—John S. Hall

"*Oscar Caliber Gun* explores the junction where the teeth of the daily grind sink into the day-dream't certainties of life's true bell-head sounds. Editor Sander Hicks has turned up another young novel to sit beside Jordan Green's *Terra Firma, U.S.A.* on the shelf of modern youth-lit."

—Lee Ranaldo

"Understand Ray's struggle as righteous and necessary: a lone act of resistance to a movie-star's anti-war/pro-war eclecticism, to Hollywood's spinelessness. If I were Tom Cruise, I'd listen up."

—Sander Hicks

Republican Like Me
Sparrow

The Ultimate Campaign Promise:
"All slaves freed, all debts forgiven!"
Shocking Proof that Lincoln was a Marxist!
It's the poetic/political memoir of Sparrow's campaign for the '96 Republican nomination.

Available: June 15

Advertising Is Vandalism
america Hoffman

The praxis of billboard modification.
It's a full-color document, before-and-after.
The son of Abbie demonstrates and records a new radicalism:
stealthier. smarter. harder.

Available: December 1

Detachable Penis
& Other Little Stories
John S. Hall

Hall returns to print with short narrative pieces dedicated to the subversion of boredom and the patriarchy. The title track is the wildest, ontologically dangerous song to get heavy rotation on Corporate Alternative Radio.

Yes, please send me the following:

_____ Angelus Novus	$8=	_____
_____ Ripsnort	$8=	_____
_____ Cash Cow & Artanimal	$8=	_____
_____ Road Movies	$8=	_____
_____ Raven Days	$8=	_____
_____ Where To?	$8=	_____
_____ Terra Firma, U.S.A.	$8=	_____
_____ Cush	$8=	_____
_____ Jesus Was Way Cool	$8=	_____
_____ Lake Success	$8=	_____
_____ Not Sisters	$8=	_____
_____ For Conifer Fanatics	$8=	_____
_____ Online Diaries	$6=	_____
_____ Oscar Caliber Gun	$9.⁹⁵=	_____

GRAND TOTAL _____

Your name and address:

send to: Soft Skull Press • 50 East Third Street No. 5A • New York, NY 10003